Books by Dave Preston

<> <> <>

False Memory OCD:
What it is and how to recover from it

Truth be Told:
A journey from the dark side of OCD

The Little Book of OCD

False Memory OCD

What it is and how to recover from it

<> <> <>

Dave Preston

Health & Wellness – Psychology – Addictions & Recovery - OCD
Health & Wellness – Psychology – Obsessive Compulsive Disorder

Version 1.00

Available on Kindle and other devices

Designed by Dave Preston

OCD Sufferers depicted in this book have had their names and details changed to protect their identities.

To Sarah

May your nightmare soon be over.

Table of Contents

Author's Note

Most books on OCD these days, with the exception of memoirs, are written by psychologists and psychiatrists. There's good reason for that. OCD is a significant mental disorder that needs to be diagnosed by a professional and, preferably, treated by a professional. That said, the people whose lives OCD has turned upside down have knowledge about the disorder too.

I was an OCD sufferer for 40 years. I suffered terribly from multiple different kinds of obsessions along quite a few different themes. I suffered in silence. I told no one about the terrible thoughts in my head. After a mental health crisis, I sought help. After four decades, I was diagnosed with OCD, put on medications and received the proper kind of treatment for my disorder.

Today I am well. I consider myself an ex-sufferer because I no longer suffer from the disorder. Along the way, I became very educated about Obsessive Compulsive Disorder. I started my own blog where I write about OCD (www.ocdlife.ca) And I spent a lot of time on OCD forums, answering questions from sufferers, offering advice and an empathetic ear. I have amassed more than 10,000 posts on forums. I consider myself a layperson's authority on OCD.

Neither this book nor any other can replace the invaluable experience of working directly with a qualified mental health professional in developing and implementing a plan to effectively deal with OCD. I encourage everyone to seek professional help.

Dave Preston

Introduction

False Memory OCD is a specific subtype of OCD, or theme. It is not a very well known form of the disorder. Many books written on the subject of OCD do not even list False Memory as a type of OCD. Most people in the general public have never heard of it, though it is found commonly on online forums that deal with Obsessive Compulsive Disorder.

It is a devastating form of OCD that causes otherwise normal people to believe they have committed some horrendous act or even crime. Sufferers become stuck in a miasma of ruminating as they strive to find an elusive truth about whether they really did something bad or not.

Some people suffer an episode for just a few days, only for it to return some time later in a new form. Other people become stuck on one terrible thought for decades.

False Memory OCD is a terrible form of OCD that saps strength, degenerates resolve, can lead to depression and debilitates sufferers tremendously. The good news is, as with any type of OCD, False Memory OCD can be treated. People can get to a better place with this form of OCD.

Before getting into the specifics of the theme, a general overview of OCD is in order.

What is OCD?

Obsessive Compulsive Disorder is a serious but treatable mental disorder that involves persistent, negative, intrusive thoughts or images (obsessions) and repetitive acts, behaviors or rituals (compulsions).

Previously the American Psychiatric Association classified OCD as an anxiety disorder, alongside Generalized Anxiety Disorder, Panic Disorder and Social Anxiety Disorder. In the fifth edition of the Diagnostic and Statistical Manual of Mental Disorders (DSM-5), OCD is now a separate diagnosis with its own chapter, *Obsessive Compulsive and Related Disorders.*

The French once called OCD 'la folie de doute', which translates to 'the doubting disease'. They had it right. OCD involves obsessions and compulsions where doubt reigns supreme. Why does a man wash his hands 50 times a day? Because he doubts his hands are clean. Why does a woman check the stove is off for the tenth time in a row? Because she doubts the stove is off, no matter how many times she has checked.

The DSM, considered the gold standard diagnostic manual in North America, lists the criteria for the diagnosis of OCD:

- Presence of obsessions, compulsions or both.
- The obsessions or compulsions are time consuming (Take more than one hour per day) or cause clinically significant distress or impairment in social, occupational or other important areas of functioning.
- The symptoms are not attributable to the physiological effects of a substance (drug abuse, a medication) or another medical condition.
- The disturbance is not better explained by the symptoms of another mental disorder (Such as Generalized Anxiety Disorder).

Pretty much everyone on the planet gets intrusive thoughts. From time to time bizarre or out of place thoughts pop up in our brains. Most people are able to dismiss these thoughts as irrelevant but it is a different story for OCD sufferers. When OCD is involved, intrusive thoughts are taken as serious, alarming and in dire need of attention. Anxiety levels rise. The sufferer feels high levels of distress. In response, the sufferer performs a compulsion to try to alleviate the distress.

It should be noted that stress makes OCD symptoms worse. Everyday stress and one-off situations such as the death of a loved one, marital problems, changing schools or finding one's self out of work, can all cause OCD to seem more troublesome.

What is an obsession?

An obsession is an intrusive thought, image, impulse, urge or fear (or any combination of) that causes distress. That should be read as: *an obsession is an intrusive thought, intrusive image, intrusive impulse, intrusive urge or intrusive fear (or any combination of) that causes distress.*

What does that mean? What is intrusive? Intrusive means causing disruption through being unwelcome and uninvited. So obsessions disrupt the sufferer because the thoughts, images, impulses, urges or fears they experience are unwelcome and uninvited. OCD sufferers do not ask for obsessions and when they get them, they really do not want them.

Some people think of intrusive thoughts as being somehow different from an obsession but they are not. Intrusive thoughts are simply a type of obsession. They are also the most common type of obsession.

Another way to think of obsessions is that they are thoughts, images, impulses, urges or fears that just pop into the sufferer's head. Sufferers do not do anything to make the thoughts, etc. pop up. The obsessions just show up on their own accord, without invitation or the sufferer doing anything to make them appear.

An important thing to know about obsessions is that they are both intrusive and cause distress. It is possible to get an intrusive thought without it causing distress and, in that case, it would not be an OCD obsession.

What kind of distress do OCD sufferers experience? The majority of sufferers describe the distress they experience as anxiety. In fact, OCD is a type of anxiety disorder and the majority of sufferers do experience heightened levels of anxiety, especially immediately following an obsession. Other types of distress experienced include guilt, shame, fear and disgust.

Obsessions themselves tend not to last a long time (in fact they can be very short in duration), but they also tend to be repetitive. This is another distinction that is important – having one or two intrusive thoughts that cause distress would not qualify for a diagnosis of OCD but things become a problem when a sufferer experiences obsessions (either the same obsession, variations on a theme or over multiple themes) repeatedly.

Obsessions are not directly controllable. There has been no mechanism found that will give a sufferer the ability to directly control or stop obsessions. What can be controlled is how sufferers respond to obsessions.

There are as many types of obsessions as there are things out there that could possible freak someone out. If it could possibly cause distress (anxiety, guilt, shame, fear, disgust, etc.) then it could be an obsession.

Every website on OCD and OCD book has a list of the more common types of obsessions. Sometimes this causes a problem for some sufferers because they cannot find their very specific obsession on any list. That does not mean they are not experiencing obsessions. It simply points to lists that are not as exhaustive as the brain's ability to conjure up disturbing thoughts or images.

If you cannot find your specific obsession on a list, don't worry. Go back to the basics: Is what you are experiencing a thought, image, urge, impulse, fear (or combination thereof)? Is it intrusive (unwanted/uninvited)? Do they just pop up in your head? Do they cause you distress? Do they lead you to perform some kind of compulsion? If so, you're probably dealing with an obsession.

What is a compulsion?

A compulsion is an action, behavior, ritual or mental ritual meant to alleviate the distress caused by obsessions. It is important to note the second part of the definition: *meant to alleviate the distress caused by obsessions.* There is a reason why sufferers perform compulsions and that is to try and get rid of or negate the distress they feel when they get obsessions.

Sufferers think they have to perform compulsions in order to get relief from obsessions. Because obsessions tend to be repetitive, so are compulsions. Sufferers end up doing the same compulsion repeatedly.

Compulsions do not work; at least not in the long term. They can bring temporary relief but soon enough the obsession causing the problem crops up again, requiring another compulsion to be performed. It can become an endless cycle of obsessions and compulsions.

Actions or behaviors are specific things done by the sufferer to offset an obsession. An example of that would be washing hands after getting an obsession about contamination of the hands. A ritual would be like spending an hour before leaving the house, checking every electric appliance to make sure they are off in a systematic way. Mental rituals include having to say a positive word to negate a negative word.

Perhaps the most common compulsion among OCD sufferers is ruminating. To ruminate means to think deeply about something and not really answer or solve anything. In psychology, it means the compulsively focused attention on the symptoms of one's distress, and on its possible causes and consequences. It means to go over and over an intrusive thought and what it means without coming to a conclusion or answer.

There is something else about compulsions that everyone should know. Not only do they not work but also they backfire. Sufferers think they have to perform compulsions to alleviate the distress brought on by obsessions. However, what compulsions actually do is draw attention to the obsessions, highlighting their importance and guaranteeing the obsessions will come back, strong, in the future.

What causes OCD?

We don't know. That's the simple answer.

Research has been done on the cause of OCD but there does not seem to be one cause evident; there is no smoking gun at this point.

There is some evidence that levels of the neurotransmitter serotonin in the brain have something to do with OCD. Indeed, many sufferers who take an SSRI (Selective Serotonin Reuptake Inhibitor) are helped to varying degrees. Then there are people who aren't. Still others are helped by taking an SSRI and an anti-psychotic (which regulates other neurotransmitters in the brain), but not everyone who takes that combination sees a significant reduction in OCD symptoms.

Brain scans have shown that certain regions of the brains of OCD sufferers are hyperactive. Whether this means there is a genetic predisposition to OCD or it is caused by a learned response remains unclear.

Some children exhibit signs of OCD after a severe infection such as strep. This is called Pediatric Autoimmune Neuropsychiatric Disorders Associated with Streptococcal infection (PANDAS).

The jury is still out on whether environment has anything to do with OCD and it is not yet clear how much a role genetics plays in the formation of the disorder.

Regardless the cause of the disorder, it is known what works to help people tame their OCD.

OCD severity

OCD comes in different levels of severity, based on the effects of obsessions and compulsions on daily living.

Severity in OCD does not refer to the type of obsessions a sufferer has. This is a misguided belief that has cropped up on the Web where some people promote the idea that some types of obsessions are worse than other obsessions. In reality, any type of obsession can be just as bad as or worse than any other.

OCD ranges from mild to moderate, severe to extreme. Those with mild forms of OCD are affected minimally by the disorder and tend to lead productive lives. Those with extreme forms of the disorder suffer debilitating consequences. Some people end up confined to their homes or even one or two rooms for many years, unable to function at work or socially, because of their OCD.

The severity of OCD can be rated by a sufferer, either on his/her own or with the assistance of a mental health professional. Google 'YBOCS' and click on one of the links. The YBOCS includes a rating scale to determine how mild or severe a case of OCD is present. It can be a valuable tool to the sufferer.

How common is OCD?

At one time OCD was considered a rare disorder, likely due to misdiagnoses by untrained healthcare professionals and due to reluctance by sufferers to talk about their symptoms. Trying to figure out how many people out there have Obsessive Compulsive Disorder can be a daunting task. Many studies have been conducted and few come up with the same number.

Studies show that between one and three percent of the population will have OCD at some point in their lives. On average, two per cent of any population has OCD. That works out to one in every 50 people.

That translates into more than 140 million worldwide, more than six million in the United States, 1.3 million in Great Britain and 700,000 in Canada.

The reason that it is difficult to pin down a more precise number is that OCD tends to be under-reported. It can take 10 to 15 years or more from the onset of symptoms for sufferers to seek help. In addition, many sufferers feel afraid, embarrassed, even shameful about their symptoms, leading to them trying to keep their obsessions and compulsions a secret. This causes delays in receiving treatment.

What is False Memory OCD?

False Memory OCD is a specific OCD theme that differs from other themes in that the sufferer perceives intrusive thoughts as memories or has a difficult time differentiating between an intrusive thought and a memory. While some other OCD themes concentrate on the possibility that the sufferer might do something bad in the future, the essence of False Memory OCD is that the sufferer believes he/she has already done something bad.

It is unknown what percentage of people with OCD suffers from False Memory OCD. It is commonly discussed on online forums and there are examples of False Memory sufferers on the World Wide Web.

This OCD theme comes in varying degrees of severity. It ranges from troublesome thoughts that bother the sufferer mildly to having profound effects on the lives of sufferers.

False Memory Obsessions

Obsessions with False Memory OCD come in the form of intrusive thoughts that are mistakenly taken as memories. These intrusive thoughts cause a fair degree of alarm, disgust, shame, guilt and fear.

The intrusive thoughts are always in the form where a sufferer believes he/she has done something catastrophically bad or illegal and against their own moral compass. Usually the sufferer knows exactly where and when the alleged act took place.

Types of obsessions vary but include:

- The sufferer believes he/she committed adultery.
- The sufferer believes he/she committed sexual abuse against another adult or child.
- The sufferer believes he/she committed murder.

False Memory OCD intrusive thoughts can be vague, such as, "I killed someone last year at a bar," or they can be very specific, such as, "I had sex with a coworker in the bathroom stall of O'Leary's Pub on Saturday night. The degree of detail the sufferer believes he/she knows has no bearing on the truthfulness of the intrusive thought. They are all false.

The intrusive thought that so bothers people with this OCD theme can first become apparent immediately after some event, the next day, several days or weeks later or six months or a year after the event. There is no correlation between when the intrusive thought surfaces to its trueness. They are all false, no matter when the intrusive thought comes alive.

Some people with False Memory OCD have obsessions that come and go with little rhyme or reason as to why. One day they are consumed by one intrusive thought and a week later a different intrusive thought grabs hold and pushes the previous one to the back burner. For other people, one intrusive thought becomes all-consuming. The same intrusive thought can haunt these people for years or even decades. The length of time an intrusive thought bothers a sufferer has no correlation to the trueness of the thought. False Memory OCD intrusive thoughts are not true.

Some people with False Memory OCD experience ongoing intrusive thoughts that vary little from the original. The intrusive thought stays about the same after weeks and months. Others experience intrusive thoughts that morph over time. Often this is because of incessant rumination and other compulsions. Since the 'memory' is not a memory at all but rather just an untrue thought, the brain can conjure up any version it likes at any time.

False Memory Perceptions

People with False Memory OCD perceive their intrusive thoughts as real. There is nothing about the thoughts that seems fake or made up.

The intrusive thoughts are perceived as memories. Even when a sufferer has previously suffered another form of OCD and fully understands what intrusive thoughts are, he/she will still perceive the intrusive thoughts about doing something bad as a memory and not as an intrusive thought.

Generally speaking, False Memory OCD sufferers overall perceive themselves as nice people, yet they can easily get to a point where they believe they were capable of committing the horrible act their thoughts tell them they did.

False Memory Compulsions

Like with all forms of OCD, those who suffer from False Memory perform compulsions to try to alleviate the distress caused by obsessions. Common types of compulsions with this theme include:

- Ruminating. This is going over the intrusive thoughts in the mind, again and again, trying to solve them, figure them out or prove them true or false. This is typically the biggest compulsion committed by False Memory OCD sufferers. Often ruminating is done every day, sometimes nonstop, for weeks, months or years. The general purpose behind the ruminating is to flesh out the so-called memory, to try to achieve certainty about the thoughts and to resolve the ever-present problem of believing something bad happened with the sufferer's sense of self (I'm a good person so how could I do such a bad thing?)

- Reassurance seeking. This can involve repeatedly asking family members and friends if they feel the sufferer capable of doing something bad. It can also involve repeatedly asking people who were at the event or night in question whether anything untoward took place. Some sufferers who know they may be suffering from OCD will repeatedly ask others if they are sure if OCD is the problem.

- Looking for evidence. Sufferers have revisited 'the scene of the crime' to see if there is any evidence of something bad happening and have even gone so far as to request copies of video surveillance to see if the crime had been recorded.

- Checking. Often sufferers will scour all forms of media, looking for stories that confirm they did something bad. For instance, someone who believes they murdered someone and discarded the body will constantly check media reports to see if a body was discovered. Another form of a checking compulsion is to check repeatedly cell phones/email to see if someone has sent a message about the alleged crime/bad event, especially if the message could come from the alleged victim of the crime.

- Confessing. Though it rarely goes that far, some sufferers deeply consider going to the police to confess their crime and turn themselves in. More often, sufferers will confide in a close friend or family member, believing they must confess what they did. Often the motive behind confessing is to receive some kind of reassurance that the sufferer is not a bad person or reassurance that the sufferer is justified in feeling the way they do.

False Memory Facts

There are some commonalities among cases of False Memory OCD. They include:

- There is never any real evidence that a catastrophically bad event took place, though the sufferer will often rely on the fact that they have a 'memory' of the act being committed as proof that the act did take place.

- More often than not, the intrusive thought involves a night that included drinking... Sometimes to excess. Drinking is not a prerequisite to having this theme but it does seem to be causal for some people. This may be because those who drink, especially a lot, are susceptible to not remembering everything that took place, putting them in a unique position to have a simple, intrusive thought misinterpreted as a memory.

- Sufferers of this OCD theme do not typically like to talk about the specifics of their memories, partly out of shame and partly out of a fear of being found out and arrested or abandoned by loved ones.

- Even when there is sound evidence against the bad event occurring, sufferers believe that there must have been way for it to happen. They will often ruminate endlessly, trying to figure out how to make contrarian evidence fit with the intrusive thought.

Michael's Story

Michael is 34-years-old and lives in the Midwest of the United States. Ever since he was a teenager, he has had some strange thoughts and done some strange things. The thoughts and behaviors didn't bother him too much but they were there and he often wondered what they meant.

One Friday night, Michael went to a bar with several friends from work. The bar was just off an Interstate highway, and nestled next to a meandering river. Michael had a few drinks, ate some appetizers for supper and had a great time with his friends, laughing and telling stories. Then he had a few more drinks.

The next morning, Michael woke up with a bit of a hangover – evidence that he had overdone it the night before. He shook his head, got out of bed and headed to the kitchen to make coffee. As he stood next to the counter waiting for the coffee to brew, a flash of a thought shot through Michael's mind. It was a brief thought that something bad had happened the previous night. The thought came with a sick feeling in his stomach. Suddenly Michael felt flushed and uneasy.

Michael immediately started thinking about the night before, trying to piece together what went on. He remembered going to the bar, meeting his friends, drinking, laughing, having a good time. But there were holes in his memory. For some reason, it dawned on Michael that those holes were crucially important and contained some devastating news.

As he drank his coffee, Michael wracked his brain, trying to remember more detail about the night in question. He could remember some things but he couldn't remember everything and that deeply troubled him. Suddenly a new thought took hold, that Michael had done something bad at the bar. It dawned on Michael that he had killed someone the previous night. He was horrified.

It felt so real. It felt so right. Inside, Michael felt that it must be true.

Mortified, Michael ran to the TV and turned it on. He found a local station broadcasting a news report and he watched intently. He just knew there would be a story about a body being discovered at the bar. One story after another went by but there was no story about a body. Fearing that he had missed what must have been a lead story, Michael vowed to watch the news again from the beginning later that day.

Shaking, Michael checked his phone to see if any of his friends had sent him a message about the body and the murder. Seeing none, he began pacing his living room, wracking his brain, trying to remember more detail about the previous night.

Details were sketchy and blurry. Michael did remember going to the washroom and it dawned on him that he must have killed the person at that time.

The phone rang and a jumpy Michael hesitantly picked it up and answered. The caller was one of Michael's friends from the night before.

"What a blast we had!" exclaimed Phil.

"Yeah I guess," said Michael.

"We've got to do that more often, though I could do without the headache I've got," said Phil.

"Me too," said Michael, who steeled himself for what he was about to ask. "Did anything happen last night?"

"What do you mean?" asked Phil.

"I don't know. Anything bad? I just have this feeling that something awful might have happened last night," said Michael.

Phil chuckled. "Not that I know of."

The conversation drifted into women at the bar, who was drinking what and how much work would be waiting come Monday. Eventually Phil said goodbye and the call ended.

Michael felt confused. How could he remember killing someone the night before yet Phil didn't say anything about it? Michael went for a shower.

Twenty minutes later, Michael found himself pacing the living room again. He tried and tried to remember more about the night at the bar. He remembered drinking, laughing, talking, and the trip to the washroom... And the body. Yes, Michael could remember seeing a body, though he couldn't tell who it was. He couldn't describe the person if he had to, but there was definitely a body.

Michael shook uncontrollably. He sat on the couch, stared off into space and went over the night in his mind, repeatedly.

Later that day, the local news ran again. Michael watched the whole broadcast. There was no mention of a body found at the bar.

"I'm sure I killed someone and I'm sure there was a body," Michael said to himself.

He checked his phone again for messages. There was none. Feeling frustrated, Michael grabbed his wallet and keys and ran out to his car and drove to the bar. Sitting in the parking lot, he could plainly see there were no cops present, no police tape strung up around the bar.

"What is going on?" Michael muttered.

Taking in the scene, Michael's eyes spied big cottonwood trees behind the property, demarking the space between a small field and the river on the other side.

"I put the body in the river," Michael muttered.

He was sure of it. Michael suddenly knew that after he killed whoever it was, he had dragged the body behind the bar, through the small field, past the cottonwoods and to the river. He realized that's why there was no news report. The body hadn't been found.

More flashing thoughts shot through Michael's brain: a body, the river, pitch black out, a knife, a gun, a knife, blood...

Michael raced home, threw open the front door and ran into his bedroom. He grabbed the clothes he had worn the night before and began frantically searching. His shirt showed no bloodstains. His pants were clean. So were his socks and underwear.

"It doesn't make sense," Michael said to himself.

For the rest of the day, Michael sat and thought. He thought about what he could remember and he thought very hard to remember what was in the holes in his memory. He shook with fright knowing he had killed someone and soon the body would be discovered and an investigation would start. He considered going to the local sheriff's office to turn himself him.

Day after day, Michael watched the news. There were never any reports of anyone missing. There were never any reports of a body being found.

Day after day, Michael sat and thought. Even when he wasn't thinking, and doing something else, his mind would wander to the night at the bar. He couldn't figure out why there was no evidence but his thoughts were evidence enough; people don't make up killing someone. Michael truly believed he must have done something awful because his brain kept generating thoughts about it.

Michael called all his friends who were at the bar that night. At first, he asked them if anything bad happened. After several calls each, Michael became more insistent, asking if there had been fight, if Michael was away from the group for any length of time, if he seemed off to any of the friends. Michael was rebuked at every turn. No one seemed to know what he was talking about.

The thoughts were relentless. Michael got no peace. If he wasn't getting thoughts firing in his mind about killing someone that night at the bar, he was scouring his memory, looking for evidence or trying to figure out if he was capable of doing such a horrendous thing.

Weeks went by. Then months. No evidence of a killing or a body surfaced. Despite that, Michael was sure he had killed someone. He couldn't shake the feeling. He couldn't shake the thoughts. He knew in his heart that he was doomed to go to prison. His personal life suffered. His work suffered. Michael withdrew from life but he relentlessly thought and thought.

OCD treatment

With the exception of OCD brought on by PANDAS (which is treated typically with a regimen of antibiotics), the treatment found to be most effective in treating OCD, and considered to be the gold standard treatment for the disorder, is Cognitive Behavioral Therapy (CBT) in conjunction with Exposure and Response Prevention (ERP), with or without medications.

OCD is chronic. That means it persists or keeps coming back. Left unchecked OCD will fester and worsen. It can become all consuming. That is why it is very important for the sufferer to start getting help the moment they've figured out they might be dealing with the disorder.

Just as people with diabetes can learn to manage their disease through diet and exercise, people with OCD can learn to manage their disorder so that it does not adversely affect their daily living and improve their quality of life. No matter the severity of OCD present, improvement is possible. Some people have been able to recover completely from their disorder to the point where they consider themselves ex-sufferers.

The best way to get on the road to recovery is to see a mental health professional for a diagnosis and to access CBT/ERP. A discussion about medications will likely happen. The first step is usually to see a general practitioner.

Some people choose to begin their recovery on their own, to varying degrees of success. The best outcomes are realized when a professional sets up a plan of action with the sufferer and the sufferer works hard to meet the goals in the plan.

It is important that a sufferer contemplating setting out on the road to recovery becomes educated about OCD (that's why you're reading this book!) and about their OCD theme, including the recommended treatment. Not all healthcare professionals can recognize the symptoms of OCD, including obsessions and compulsions, and may not know where to send the sufferer for help. In this case, the sufferer, with foreknowledge, can help guide the process along.

Recovering from OCD is not a sprint; it's a marathon. There is no quick fix for OCD. It typically takes years for things to get bad enough that a sufferer will ask for help and it's not going to be fixed overnight. Recovering from OCD takes education, determination, a proper plan, time and hard work.

Although not a treatment for OCD, per se, many people find relaxation therapies and/or mindfulness to be helpful during the recovery process.

False Memory OCD Treatment

Before discussing treatment for False Memory OCD, one has to look at the challenge of getting sufferers of this particular theme to the point where they realize the problem is not what they think and that it is treatable.

False Memory OCD sufferers perceive their intrusive thoughts as memories. Much of their gut tells them that they did something terrible, even illegal. Unless they are aware of OCD and False Memory OCD, they aren't going to perceive that what they are going through is symptoms of a treatable mental disorder. Fortunately, for many sufferers, there has been a history of OCD relevant to them that they can start with. They know they have OCD and it's not too big a leap to consider the possibility that what they are currently dealing with is just another form of the disorder.

Also challenging is the fact that, although sufferers will sometimes go to unusual lengths to seek evidence and reassurance from others, they are usually loathe to openly discuss their thoughts to others, out of fear of imprisonment and abandonment.

Luckily, the World Wide Web can be a good source of information and stories about False Memory OCD. Once a sufferer realizes there is such a thing, they can then begin to explore for information about it and broaden their understanding of the theme.

Once the initial hurdle of theme recognition is dealt with, the treatment of False Memory OCD is the same as other themes of Obsessive Compulsive Disorder. Cognitive Behavioral Therapy is still the front line treatment, along with ERP (Exposure and Response Prevention).

Medications

Whether to go on medications for OCD is a personal choice best left to the sufferer and his/her GP or psychiatrist. Knowledge is power. There are some facts about medications everyone should know.

Different people respond differently to OCD medications. There is no hard and fast rule as to how medications will help, if at all, anyone who takes them. It isn't helpful to ask people what medications they take or how they respond to them because everyone is different. What works for one person may not work for another.

Some people find common medications take the edge off anxiety, allowing them to concentrate on a treatment plan based on CBT/ERP. Some people do not respond at all to medications, even after trying a number of them. Still others find their symptoms (frequency and severity of obsessions, need to perform compulsions) diminished moderately to greatly while taking medications.

Medications come with side effects. Some people barely notice side effects while others have such severe reactions to a medication that they have to stop taking their medications. Others experience side effects that subside over time. Always be aware of the likely side effects you could experience if you are considering going on an OCD medication.

Only taking medications to recover from OCD is not recommended. The web is replete with stories of OCD sufferers who took medications, got better to some degree, and then went off the medications only to find they were right back to square one again. Medications do not cure OCD but they can help for some people. Generally speaking, medications tend to help reduce overall anxiety, which can help sufferers to better engage with therapy.

The most commonly prescribed medication for OCD is anti-depressants, notably a class of anti-depressant called SSRIs (Selective Serotonin Reuptake Inhibitors). There are quite a number of them and they include:

Generic Name (Trade Name)
- Citalopram (Cipramil/Celexa)
- Escitalopram (Cipralex)
- Fluoxetine (Prozac)
- Fluvaxamine (Luvox/Faverin)
- Paroextine (Paxil/Seroxat)
- Sertraline (Lustral/Zoloft)

A less commonly prescribed medication for OCD is the non-selective Serotonin Reuptake Inhibitor clomipramine (Anafranil). There tends to be more side effects with this drug than SSRIs and it affects more neurotransmitters than just serotonin.

Some psychiatrists prescribe an anti-psychotic along with an SSRI in the treatment of OCD. Anti-psychotics include Rispiradone (risperdal) and Abilify (aripiprazole). Once again, these drugs come with possible side effects and knowledge is power.

Cognitive Behavioral Therapy

The gold standard treatment for OCD is CBT (Cognitive Behavioral Therapy) with ERP (Exposure and Response Prevention), with or without medications. Studies suggest that 75 per cent of those sufferers who received CBT are significantly helped. There are no risks or side effects to this form of therapy when it comes to treating OCD.

CBT is a combination of two types of therapy: Cognitive therapy, which looks to change the way a sufferer thinks; and behavioral therapy, which looks to change the way a sufferer behaves. ERP is a special type of behavioral therapy.

The goal of CBT is not to learn how not to have intrusive thoughts/obsessions. In fact, that would be pointless, since everyone gets intrusive thoughts. They happen all the time. What CBT is for is to learn to react differently to the obsessions that will come up in the future. CBT teaches the sufferer that the thoughts themselves are not the problem; it is what the sufferer does with the thoughts and how they react to them that is the problem.

From a cognitive perspective, a sufferer can begin to learn to think about intrusive thoughts differently. Those thoughts, which used to be taken as being extremely negative, can be looked at as irrelevant, meaningless mind junk that can be dismissed without worry.

Cognitively, it is better to take a non-committed attitude about obsessions than it is to do the usual and argue against what the obsession stands for. For example, if a sufferer gets an intrusive thought that he could stab his partner with a knife, the usual result might be to argue internally that that would never happen, that the sufferer would never harm another person. All that does is brings attention to the obsession, guaranteeing it will come back in the future. Instead, the sufferer should think, immediately after the obsession pops up, that maybe they will stab their partner tonight. Then leave the whole matter alone.

With cognitive therapy, sufferers can learn that intrusive thoughts are just thoughts and don't mean anything. They are simply brain noise that pops up from time to time and they can be safely ignored as irrelevant.

From a behavioral perspective, a sufferer can learn that they don't have to behave the way they normally do every time an obsession strikes. How do they normally behave? They perform compulsions. The behavioral therapy side of CBT teaches the sufferer it's okay to not perform compulsions. ERP is about directly challenging OCD while practicing not performing compulsions.

Cognitive Therapy for False Memory OCD

People with False Memory OCD perceive their intrusive thoughts as memories. They need to change that perception. Intrusive thoughts are just thoughts; they are not memories and there is nothing real about them. Being exposed to other stories about False Memory OCD can be a good thing because it teaches the sufferer that they are not alone, that there are others out there suffering from the same thing and that it all falls under the OCD umbrella. The reason it's called False Memory OCD is that the 'memory' is 'false'. There is nothing true about it.

It can be a hard pill to swallow for some people to admit they have a mental disorder. For others it can be freeing, knowing there is an identifiable reason why they are the way they are. The important thing to remember is that OCD is a treatable mental disorder. Having OCD is not a life sentence. People can and do recover from OCD and False Memory OCD.

Everyone gets intrusive thoughts. With people who have OCD, something is amiss and along with the intrusive thought, the brain pushes the panic button, causing the sufferer to stand up and take notice and do something about the thoughts. It isn't the thoughts themselves that are the problem. How the sufferer reacts to the thoughts creates the problem. False Memory OCD sufferers get intrusive thoughts that they did something bad and they react by doing compulsions. They can learn that it is their reaction to the thoughts is the problem and they don't have to react the same old way anymore.

Sufferers can begin to realize that those 'memories' they are so worried about are actually just intrusive thoughts that it's okay to ignore. They're mental chaff they don't want but there's no harm to them. They are just samples of the 10,000 or so thoughts the typical person has every day. They don't mean anything, they aren't representative of anything, they aren't threatening and they can be dismissed as irrelevant.

Doubt is a big part of OCD and False Memory OCD is no exception. Sufferers feel doubtful about their memories, they experience doubts that they are the good people they always thought they were and they doubt their ability to get past the intrusive thoughts. Sufferers often go through months or years of chronic doubt. Doubt doesn't make the thoughts true. Doubt can be overcome with positive thoughts.

Cognitive therapy. Thinking differently. Sufferers should look at their doubts, write them down, turn those doubts around and come up with new ways of thinking. *I am a bad person* can become *I am a good person. I killed someone* can become *I treat people with dignity and respect.* It's about changing perceptions. Some people write positive messages to themselves in a book that's read every day or on sticky notes stuck to the bathroom mirror so they can be reviewed at the beginning of every day.

Ask a False Memory OCD sufferer why they spend so much time ruminating and doing other compulsions and he/she will probably respond something akin to, "I'm trying to figure it out for sure." The search for certainty is a huge part of this theme. Sufferers never seem to be 100 per cent sure they've done something terribly bad. They may be fairly confident they did, but they are never totally convinced. Hence the search for certainty. It's a search that can never be concluded successfully.

False Memory OCD sufferers will never find the certainty they seek. It doesn't matter how much thinking and ruminating they do, they will never reach a point where they are completely certain, one way or the other. It doesn't matter if there is a total lack of evidence that anything bad happened; sufferers continue to believe they probably did something bad. Cognitive Therapy can teach sufferers to give up their search for certainty and live with uncertainty gracefully. In fact, it is critical that sufferers give up the search for certainty. They have to surrender to the unknown and be satisfied with it. Only then can they begin to move forward.

Sufferers will often complain that they must achieve perfect clarity, that anything else is dooming them to a life of uncertainty where they believe they have done something terrible. That is not true. They can, with the proper therapy, learn to cope and successfully live without clarity. They can achieve a place with their thinking where they simply don't care about the intrusive thoughts anymore, where they go on with their lives without ever finding the magic clarity they sought for so long.

Stopping False Memory OCD Compulsions

No one ever recovered from OCD while continuing to do compulsions.

Read it, think about it, understand it.

Uninformed sufferers think obsessions are the bad guy because they can cause such a visceral reaction. However, compulsions are the real problem when it comes to OCD.

Compulsions are done to try to alleviate some of the distress caused by obsessions but they don't really work out that way. When compulsions are done, they bring attention to the obsessions, they cement the obsessions in the mind and cause obsessions to come back more often and more forcefully than before.

As hard as it may seem, compulsions have to be stopped. Sufferers cannot directly stop intrusive thoughts from happening but they do have control over compulsions. Some compulsions seem automatic; they seem to happen all by themselves. That is in part due to conditioning. Sufferers rely on compulsions to get them through the tough times and they teach themselves to do them. What can be taught can be untaught. Compulsions must stop.

The first step is to figure out what compulsions are being performed. There is a list of possible compulsions near the beginning of this book. There may be others that are being done. Any act, behavior, ritual or mental ritual that is done after intrusive thoughts pop up is a compulsion. With False Memory OCD, the most common and biggest compulsion is ruminating.

Ruminating means to go over a thought repeatedly in the mind without ever really getting anywhere with the work. It is taking the intrusive thought, breaking it down, trying to figure out what it means, analyzing the thought, trying to determine if it's true or not, and on and on.

Ruminating can be stopped but it is hard. The process is straightforward. The sufferer must first know what ruminating is. Then they must be able to determine that they are doing it at the time. Next, the sufferer must stop the action. Then the sufferer needs to shift their attention onto something else (whatever they happen to be doing at the time is fine.) Sometimes ruminating becomes all encompassing, so a complete shift is in order. A sufferer might decide to get up and go for a walk, trying to concentrate on the view around them, what they see, what they feel, what they hear. It's an exercise in shifting the attention from the ruminating to the world around, giving the mind a break in the process.

It takes lots of practice to stop ruminating. It isn't easy and there will be pitfalls along the way. Some days it will be just too hard to stop. A bad day happens. There will be a couple of good days and then it all comes crashing down again. It's about keeping going. Putting one foot in front of the other and slowly trying again.

Compulsions do not have to be stopped cold turkey. It can be a gradual, less painful exercise. For instance, a sufferer might have a compulsion of reassurance seeking from family and friends. He/she might ask continually if they are a good person (to counteract the intrusive thoughts that they've done something bad). The sufferer can gradually work on stopping. A long-term goal can be set for how much reassurance should be sought a month from now. (In this case, none would be a good goal). Day one could be to cut down from continual reassurance seeking to only seeking reassurance four times. Day three could be to cut down to only two instances of reassurance seeking. Day eight could see only one bout of reassurance seeking sought. And on and on until, slowly, the compulsion is eliminated or at least severely curtailed.

Not doing compulsions, at first, causes anxiety levels to rise. This should be expected. OCD sufferers condition themselves to react to obsessions by performing compulsions. Suddenly stopping or delaying compulsions will cause anxiety to go up because the usual release mechanism is no longer being done. However, typically anxiety levels come down in short order. Over time, sufferers will learn that their anxiety levels may go up but they come down on their own without having to do compulsions.

People who have successfully accomplished the goal of eliminating compulsions notice that their intrusive thoughts come less frequently and, for those that still come through, they are weaker and seem less threatening. This is the prize at the end of the stopping-compulsion rainbow.

Exposure and Response Prevention

ERP is widely hailed as a breakthrough therapy for the treatment of OCD. It goes hand in hand with cognitive therapy and the practice of eliminating compulsions. It is all about challenging OCD directly.

ERP is composed of two parts: the exposure, where the sufferer exposes himself/herself to the subject of intrusive thoughts, and response prevention, where the sufferer practices not doing compulsions.

A qualified therapist will usually help a sufferer develop a hierarchy of obsessions and compulsions. This is done by listing out all the obsessions and compulsions that need to be dealt with and then ranking them on the amount of anxiety/distress caused by each obsession or the anxiety/distress the sufferer feels would be caused by not performing each compulsion.

With a ranked hierarchy (from least anxiety provoking to most anxiety provoking) in hand, the sufferer can begin ERP on the items at the bottom of the list first, tackling the easier obsessions/compulsions to start with.

For each item on the list, the sufferer exposes himself/herself to the obsession and then practices not performing the usual compulsion associated with that compulsion. This is done repeatedly until, over time, the sufferer experiences less and less anxiety doing so. Eventually the sufferer barely notices anxiety/distress after an exposure. At that point, it's time to move up one step on the list to the next obsession/compulsion.

Take the case of a sufferer who can't stand to touch 'dirty' things. If he does, he washes his hands for 10 minutes at a time, sometimes with bleach. The sufferer would make a list of things he would try to avoid touching. Perhaps one is a garbage can. As part of ERP, the sufferer touches a garbage can (the exposure) and then sits and waits without washing his hands (response prevention). Repeated sessions of this should lessen his anxiety about touching garbage cans. Next, the sufferer could up the ante, so to speak, to rubbing his hand all over a garbage can and then rubbing his face with the same hand (exposure). Again, the sufferer would have to forego washing his hands or at least delaying it for a specified time (response prevention).

ERP is typically done at a specified time, after work each day, for instance. The more ERP is done, the faster it will work. Sufferers should know there is a limit to the amount of exposures they can do before they need a break. Typically, exposures are done perhaps once per day until the exposures no longer raise anxiety levels significantly. A well-motivated sufferer might decide to do exposures twice a day.

The idea with ERP is to cause anxiety levels to rise with the exposure, then sit and wait for anxiety levels to lower back down to near normal levels, without doing compulsions in the process. When anxiety has lowered, the ERP session is over. In time, the sufferer should notice that their anxiety peaks at a lower and lower level and their anxiety returns to a normal level in a shorter and shorter time-period. This is evidence that ERP is working.

Therapists will often give the sufferer a chart to work with when doing ERP. Columns are labeled for date, ERP start time, starting anxiety level, peak anxiety level, ERP end time and end anxiety level. Anxiety levels are rated on a scale of 1 to 10, 1 being completely relaxed and 10 being near panic attack. The sufferer records the necessary information on the chart and can see, over repeated exposures, whether they are improving.

ERP for False Memory OCD

To get the best possible outcome from ERP, sufferers should work with a qualified professional who knows how to teach and monitor the therapy. An OCD therapist can sit down with a sufferer and design a plan that takes into account his/her obsessions and compulsions and design an ERP program that will produce the best results.

The first step is to figure out exactly what the obsession or intrusive thought is that is bothering the sufferer. This is what will form the exposure part of ERP.

The second step is to be aware of what the typical compulsions are when the obsession strikes. This needs to be known because the sufferer will be trying to refrain from doing those compulsions (response prevention) and will need to know what to watch out for.

ERP for False Memory OCD differs from ERP for some other forms of OCD. The exposure is not a matter of touching a garbage can, for instance. There is no object to touch before practicing not doing compulsions. Instead, the sufferer must expose him/herself to the actual intrusive thought that is causing the problem. This can be done in one of several different ways. Every therapist is going to have his or her favorite ways of conducting ERP. Suggestions include:

- Writing down the intrusive thought on a piece of paper, repeatedly.
- Making a recording of the sufferer stating the intrusive thought repeatedly and then listening to the recording.
- Standing in front of a mirror and stating the intrusive thought repeatedly.

For example, a woman with False Memory OCD, when it is time to do ERP, might read from a prepared piece of paper that has the intrusive thought written down. It might say something like, "I had sex with a male coworker in a bathroom stall on the fifth floor of my office building at the Christmas party last December." She would say it to herself repeatedly. She is saying aloud the intrusive thought that has bothered her. Hopefully (yes, hopefully!) her anxiety level goes up hearing herself state her intrusive thought. After several repetitions, she stops and then works on the response prevention part of

ERP, which is all about not performing compulsions. She noted with her therapist that her big compulsion was ruminating so that's what she watches out for. She lets the intrusive thought she's vocalized float around in her head and she works hard to not ruminate over it. She leaves the thought alone, refusing to get into a mind debate about the thought. It takes some time, but slowly her anxiety level lessens and returns to a near normal level. The ERP session is then over.

Another example is a man who believes he touched a child inappropriately at a birthday party making a tape recording of his voice. On the recording, the man has stated, "I sexually abused a child at a birthday party in July," repeatedly. When it is time for an ERP session, the man listens to the tape and then works to not do his usual compulsions, which include ruminating and asking his wife and other relatives for reassurance that he is not a bad person and incapable of harming a child.

Relaxation and mindfulness

Stress makes OCD worse. It makes sense then, that reducing stress can make OCD better.

Relaxation and mindfulness do not cure OCD. They don't directly make obsessions, or the need to perform compulsions, go away. However, learning to relax and be in the moment can make for a relaxed, less stressed person and that can have benefits when it comes to dealing with OCD.

Resources to learn relaxation and mindfulness are nearly endless. Lessons abound on the web. YouTube has many videos that can guide you through exercises. There are many books on the subject. Check with your GP or local mental health organization to find out if there are relaxation groups in your area.

How to approach a GP

Talking about your OCD to your doctor can be a scary proposition. Many people find it incredibly difficult to talk about the scary thoughts they have or the compulsions they feel they have to perform repeatedly. It can be extra challenging talking about obsessions that deal with sexual orientation or children and sex.

Visiting your GP to start the process toward recovery is just the first step. Your GP doesn't need to know everything about your OCD since he/she will be recommending you to some kind of mental health service or therapist. Though many GPs have some experience dealing with OCD issues, not every GP has experience with every possible type of obsession and compulsion.

You can start by simply saying, "I think I have OCD," or "I think my child has OCD."

You can go a little further by explaining the theme of obsessions you or your child has, without going into specifics about the type of obsessions experienced. You can also talk broadly about the types of compulsions present.

The idea is to give your doctor enough information so he/she will know what to do – namely get you an appointment with someone who can help you.

Recovery Challenges

Recovery from False Memory OCD is not a linear process. There will be pitfalls along the way. Sufferers will have good days and bad days. Things will go well, then the intrusive thoughts strike hard and a setback occurs. This is normal and should be expected. When challenges occur, it is important to stop, regroup, review the plan and start out again. Put one foot in front of the other and recovery will continue.

Because False Memory OCD sufferers perceive their obsessions as memories and not the intrusive thoughts they are, they are prone to slipping back into the thinking that the thoughts are real, the bad thing really did happen and they are a terrible person. This is where a leap of faith is required.

Sufferers do not, in the beginning, necessarily need to believe their thoughts are just intrusive thoughts and not real. However, they do need to take a leap of faith that the problem is all OCD, and then do the hard work necessary to recover. It is not an easy leap to take, especially when the mind is constantly saying the feared event actually happened. Nevertheless, a leap of faith is needed. It will help sufferers to engage more easily with therapy and continue their journeys to recovery.

Conclusion

False Memory OCD is a terrible form of OCD to go through. Living with it can be like finding yourself in mental quicksand, stuffed full of terrible thoughts, crushing doubt and high anxiety. Sufferers can find themselves in a near constant state of intrusive thoughts followed by compulsions for weeks, months or years with no break until steps are taken to get help.

False Memory OCD can be beaten. It is a struggle, it is challenging, it is hard, but ultimately it is relatively simple to recover from this OCD theme. It takes a lot of commitment by the sufferer to follow a program that includes cognitive therapy, stopping compulsions and ERP. It is a slow process but it is one where sufferers can see the benefits early on. They must commit to the process and do the hard work necessary to succeed.

About the author

Dave Preston is an author, freelance writer and small town journalist. *False Memory OCD: What it is and how to recover from it* is his third book on Obsessive Compulsive Disorder. He lives in British Columbia's Okanagan Valley with his wife Jackie, his son and the indelible memory of Miss Kitty.

You can help

If you enjoyed this book, if it changed your mind about what OCD is, if it made you think deeply, won't you consider logging onto your favorite online book retailer and leaving a review? It both helps the author and helps other readers discover this book.

Connect Online

www.OCDLife.ca
www.twitter.com/ocdlife

Truth Be Told
A journey from the dark side of OCD

Dave Preston

Read the riveting OCD memoir today!

The story of one man's journey from the depths of mental hell to the promised light of recovery. This dramatic narrative will make readers re-evaluate what they thought they knew about OCD.

For 40 years Dave keeps his horrible intrusive thoughts a secret. A police investigation crashes his world around him. He seeks professional help. He is diagnosed with an extreme case of OCD, which answers why he had the terrible thoughts for so long but also why the police showed up at his door.

What customers are saying about Truth be Told:

"It should be required reading for anyone who dismisses OCD as a mild personality quirk, and it will connect with anyone who's suffered with this devastating illness."

"A journey from the dark side is a very apt description of one man's life-time struggle with the debilitating disorder of OCD... It is a well-written book that captures the despair accurately. In it I saw so many things that I could relate to. There were times I could have wept at the account."

"A brutally honest account of one man's struggles with OCD and the earth shattering effects it can have on the person and those around them."

"I'm sure this book and your future efforts will enlighten and help so many sufferers as well as further the cause of removing the stigma attached to mental illness in society."

Available on Amazon